Dear Grandma

Dear Grandma,

I like our new house.
It has no curtains yet.
When I went to bed,
Mum put up a sheet!
I miss you.

Love,
  Carl

Our New House

Dear Carl,

I like the plan of your house. I am making some curtains for your bedroom.

Love,
Grandma

PS I miss you, too.

Which design do you like?

Fat Cats

Dazzling
Dolphins

Farmyard Fun

Story-Book People

Dear Grandma,

I like the dazzling dolphins best!

I went to my new school today.
Mum and I walked all the way.
I have a new friend
named Ben.

Love,
   Carl

Dear Carl,

Thank you for the map. It will help me find your house when I visit you. I wish you were here with me.

Love,
Grandma

PS I am staying far away from alligators!

See You Later, Alligator
Florida, U.S.A.

9

Dear Grandma,

I like your postcard.
Can you please send me
something about Waterworld?

Mum is looking for a new job.
She wants to be a vet!

Love,
  Carl

11

Dear Carl,

When your mum was
a little girl, she loved
to play with animals!

On your next holiday,
we will go to Waterworld.

Love,
    Grandma

  PS See you soon!

Your mum!
Isn't she cute?

13

Dear Grandma,

Thank you for the photos of Mum. She has a new job at the bank. She said she liked counting money when she was a little girl, too!

I showed the Waterworld brochures at school today.

Love,
    Carl

PS See you next week!

Waterworld

Splash Out!
Join us on a wet and wild Waterworld adventure...

16

A
WANDER
IN THE
WOODS

Fictional Fun

Edited By Debbie Killingworth

First published in Great Britain in 2021 by:

Young Writers
Remus House
Coltsfoot Drive
Peterborough
PE2 9BF
Telephone: 01733 890066
Website: www.youngwriters.co.uk

Printed and bound in the UK by BookPrintingUK
Website: www.bookprintinguk.com
YB0465J

FOREWORD

Welcome, Reader!

Are you ready to take a Wander in the Woods? Then come right this way - your journey to amazing adventures awaits. It's very simple, all you have to do is turn the page and you'll be transported into a forest brimming with super stories.

Is it magic? Is it a trick? No! It's all down to the skill and imagination of primary school pupils from around the country. We gave them the task of writing a story and to do it in just 100 words! I think you'll agree they've achieved that brilliantly – this book is jam-packed with exciting and thrilling tales, and such variety too, from mystical portals to creepy monsters lurking in the dark!

These young authors have brought their ideas to life using only their words. This is the power of creativity and it gives us life too! Here at Young Writers we want to pass our love of the written word onto the next generation and what better way to do that than to celebrate their writing by publishing it in a book!

It sets their work free from homework books and notepads and puts it where it deserves to be – out in the world and preserved forever! Each awesome author in this book should be super proud of themselves, and now they've got proof of their ideas and their creativity in black and white, to look back on in years to come!

CONTENTS

Ripley Court School, Ripley

Alf Orford (10)	55
Evelyn Shaw (10)	56
Aiden Tyack-Hamadi (10)	57
Thomas Caine (10)	58
Nancy O'Rourke (9)	59
Ayesha Nagelson (10)	60
Harry Goggin (10)	61
Naina Sharma (10)	62
Juliana Lima (9)	63
Sophie Pascoe (10)	64
Katie Mathur (9)	65
James Collins (10)	66
Jasmin Knight (10)	67
James Bevan (10)	68
James Batten (9)	69
Matilda Coen (10)	70
Alexandra Mann (10)	71
Daniel Gillam (10)	72
Leo Necmi (9)	73
Callista Cumberland (11)	74
Alice Nash (10)	75
Sophia Smith (10)	76
Arthur Ogilive Smals (10)	77
Lara Bailey (10)	78
Ella Kemp (10)	79
Max Lippiett (10)	80
Emilie Dick (9)	81
Sophie Stephens (10)	82
Iris Watt (9)	83
Isabel Forwood (9)	84
Martha Wilcockson (10)	85
Jack Sparks (10)	86
Oliver Tiernan (10)	87
Oscar Gill (10)	88
Tom Douthett (10)	89
Poppy Renshaw (10)	90
Mario Valenta (10)	91
Lior Reich (9)	92
Alex Maroudas (9)	93
Daisy Constable (9)	94
Marius Boyd (10)	95
Jorja Asumang (10)	96
Alice Knight (9)	97
Pip Roberts (10)	98
Sophie Mills (10)	99
Poppy Miller (9)	100
Cameron Hermiston (11)	101
Benjamin Everitt (9)	102
Harry O'Gilvie (10)	103
Daniel Peyton (10)	104
Nate Eustace (10)	105
Tyler Engelbrecht (9)	106
Harry O'Sullivan (9)	107
Alexa France (9)	108
Tish O'Gilvie (9)	109
Toby Holdsworth (11)	110
Jessica Lush (9)	111
Daniel Bimson (9)	112
Alfie Rice (10)	113
Amy French (9)	114
Charlie Carr (11)	115
Max Ground (10)	116

Wheatlands Primary School, Redcar

Oscar Edwardson (10)	117
Lucie Scott (11)	118
Louie Bowstead (10)	119
Anya Wales (10)	120
Katie Middleton (10)	121
Jessica Buggey (10)	122
Rosie Winspear (11)	123
Katie Walker (10)	124
Ethan Robinson (10)	125
Dolly Kirwan (10)	126
Jonah Tennant (10)	127
Sam Drinkhall (10)	128
Oliver Hamilton (11)	129
Jaycie-Kay Duncan (11)	130
Gracie Mansfield (10)	131
Phoebe Webster (10)	132
Sophie Marshall (10)	133
Louis Hartley (10)	134
Theo Ward (10)	135
Alexis Tate (10)	136

Callum Clegg (11)	137
Ben Joseph Reed (10)	138
Freya Putson (11)	139
Fabio Bernard (11)	140
Annabelle Pearson (10)	141
Isaac Bilton (10)	142
Alfie McDonald (11)	143
Charlie Leach (10)	144
Ruby Hodgson (11)	145
Reece Cummings (11)	146
Lloyd Johnson (10)	147
Scarlett Scrafton (10)	148
Luca Smith (11)	149
Daniel Bryce (10)	150
Cory Noble (10)	151
Bryn Boswell (10)	152
Archie Hodgson (10)	153
Harvey Barton (11)	154
Neve Pettite (10)	155
Finley Mapplebeck (11)	156
Connor Sowerby (10)	157
Lucas Richardson (10)	158
Darcie Cook (10)	159
Scarlett Willet	160

Ysgol Melyd, Prestatyn

Maximus Roberts (9)	161
Maisie Vaughan (8)	162
Noah Davies (9)	163
Sian Owen (8)	164
Will Lamb (8)	165
Megan Duffy Hamill (9)	166
Emily Hughes (8)	167
Stanley Pope (8)	168
Kian Semple (8)	169
Elijah Jones (9)	170

THE STORIES

Wander In The Woods

In the cold, damp woods, four cousins were walking along, chatting and laughing. Suddenly, they heard strange noises. They looked around to see what was there. Nothing. They all stood still. Creepy laughs were coming from a shuddering bush ahead. They huddled up, really scared. They watched the bush and saw something white appear. A ghost jumped out and shouted, "Boo!" The cousins ran as fast as they could out of the woods. "This is why I hate the woods!" the youngest cousin shouted. It turned out it was their grandfather, who hid in the bush to scare his grandchildren!

Reuben Cooper (10)

Glory Farm Primary School, Bicester

The Wander In The Dark Woods

Once upon a time, there was a town called Nari. The children who lived in Nari were called Abigail, Bethany, Alexander and Evelyn. One day they went to the dark woods and they came across a humongous oak tree and engraved in the oak tree were the words: 'Wait for adventure'.

They went home that night and dreamt of treasure, millions and trillions waiting for them the next day. They went back the next day, waiting for their treasure but it wasn't there then they realised, it was not all about the treasure, it's about the adventure that they shared!

Abigail Burgess (9)

Glory Farm Primary School, Bicester

The Friendly Monster

There was a monster called Freddy. He was a nice monster but people didn't think so. The royal family thought he would kill them all! That was untrue, Freddy was a lovely monster but he decided to stay in his dark, wet cave. Freddie deserved more.

One day a deer stumbled across his cave and said, "Why are you here alone? Come see all the nature and animals."

So Freddy, feeling sad, stumbled along behind her. When Freddy saw the bright sun and all the lovely animals his eyes widened. Everyone just stared and then cheered and clapped Freddy on.

Amelia Gardner Delvalle (10)

Glory Farm Primary School, Bicester

The Wonder Of My Life

One wintry day, I was exploring in the dark, creepy woods, when I saw some huge, pointy footprints. I couldn't help myself... I followed them and they led me to a dragon! It had an egg curled up in its tail. The egg was all bumpy and cracked open. So I woke up the dragon and tried to explain to it that someone had stolen the baby dragon. The dragon said, "It's fine, he's probably gone to explore in the woods. That's what all new dragons do."
"I guess humans and dragons aren't so different after all!" I said surprisingly!

Madison Joiner (9)
Glory Farm Primary School, Bicester

A Walk In The Woods

One day Wolfy wandered off from his pack. First, he wandered ahead into the lush purple of Fairy Cove, where he saw mushroom houses and fireflies. Then he crossed Troll Bridge, luckily there wasn't a troll to give him a riddle so he was able to cross straight away. After crossing the bridge he walked through Dandelion Lane, admiring all the flowers. Wolfy then travelled up to Goat Mountain where the pack was out hunting. He got home just in time to have tea and he told his mum all about his exciting adventure, even though she didn't believe him.

Amelia Beart (9)

Glory Farm Primary School, Bicester

The Mysterious Camping Trip

There were four friends called Hazel, Lewis, Riley and Daisy who loved going camping. They decided they were going on a camping trip. So they packed up their stuff and headed off. When they got there, they went to set up their beds and then spent the whole day out. After a long day, they finally went to sleep, but in the middle of the night, Hazel heard a strange noise. They got up and looked around. Riley saw something behind Hazel, it was a park ranger. Daisy took a closer look and realised it was *the* missing park ranger...

Lucy Huxford (9)
Glory Farm Primary School, Bicester

The Spooky Camping Trip

There was a boy called Jake, he had a normal family. Mom, Dad, a sister called Emma and a dog. They were going on a camping trip, a normal old camping trip. They got packed and in the car for a long journey. When they finally arrived after a three-hour journey they decided to go for a walk in the lovely nature. Emma and Jake's mum and dad stopped to look at something. Emma and Jake carried on walking, they heard something and ran back screaming but it was just the dog sniffing in the bushes. Everyone laughed!

Lexie Marjoram (9)
Glory Farm Primary School, Bicester

A Wander In The Woods

There was a castle in the forest, and in that castle lived lots of animals. There were bears, one named Freddy and he was the king of the castle. He gave everyone their jobs to do. The foxes went hunting for food, the sheep made wool for blankets and the squirrels collected nuts to eat and they all got on really well. Then one misty night a pack of wolves came and tried to take over the castle. But the bear and the foxes managed to fight them off. The wolves ran off in fear and never came back.

Sam Rainbow (10)

Glory Farm Primary School, Bicester

A Wander In The Woods

One day in the woods there was a boy who was a 10-year-old orphan. He lived alone in his cabin. One day he went into the woods and heard someone. He looked closer and he was bitten by a vampire.

A week later the boy went to the city and looked for a chemist to get a cure for the bite. The doctor said he had no cure but could he come back later, and he did. The doctor said he still had no cure, so smeared garlic bread in the face of the boy to end his misery.

Charlie Honour (10)

Glory Farm Primary School, Bicester

The Watchful Tree

When I look out my window I see a tree, a tree with an owl face. He never moves, he just watches and listens to the laughter. He sits there year after year, day after day. He never comments, he just smiles and sits. He looks bare in winter and autumn but in summer and spring he's beautiful, with flowers and leaves and blossoms. I never go and fuss him, he just watches as life goes by.

Cody Alexander (9)
Glory Farm Primary School, Bicester

The Enchanted Forest

Once upon a strange time, there was a massive castle in front of the Forest of Doom. As I opened the gate, I saw many strange creatures. Dragons flying with their colossal blue wings and great white sharks leaping everywhere. Then, without me noticing, I saw a massive octopus the size of a tall building. Then I caught a glimpse of a poisonous frog on a lilypad. Snakes and octopuses were roaming the forests and soaring pelicans and dragons were soaring in the sky. Star-nosed moles were digging the ground and beavers eating, they were the best creatures!

Tomisin Oguntola (8)

Harris Primary Academy Haling Park, Croydon

The Secret Enchanted Forest

Once there was a little girl called Lily. She was walking in the forest. She found a cave in the middle of the forest. She walked in and saw a talking rabbit and an enchanted lake where she could make a wish and it would come true. She wished her mum and dad would come back from Heaven. Her brother was looking for her and saw the cave and walked in. He found his sister and said, "What're you doing talking to a rabbit?" Years later she brought her daughter to the cave to protect it from the goblin's destroyers.

Kyanne-Nadine Bennett (10)
Harris Primary Academy Haling Park, Croydon

The Mystery Half

One day a lovely family went on a spectacular trip to a forest. They looked around to see where to set up their tent. They finally found it by noon. Half of the family went hunting while the others stayed near the tent. Suddenly a spaceship sucked them up. They were very confused then an alien said, "Hello," then the family gasped and ran but it was all locked. They said, "Okay, we will drop you home after you give us a sweet." The family said okay with relief and gave them one then they got dropped off happily.

Zara Rashid (8)

Harris Primary Academy Haling Park, Croydon

Jodie And The Magical Creature

One day I decided to go to a magical forest. I thought it was a myth but when I saw all the white, delicate butterflies fluttering around my head, then I saw six bunnies building with bricks. Then I heard something strange and saw a goat, a huge goat in a cage. I went towards it and it said, "Hello."
I touched the white, fluffy goat, as soft as a pillow. It climbed out and asked me to help it get its child, then I realised it was a girl. We swooped towards her. We snatched her and, victory!

Jodie Crawford-Ackim (9)

Harris Primary Academy Haling Park, Croydon

The Missing Dog

One day the dog went missing and the owners were terrified because she was only a puppy and they were in the woods, it was also dark. Soon the owners found her collar. They called the local place and they used X-ray vision and found the dog was in the lake so they went to go save her. She was soon rescued and reunited with her owners.

Jayden James Cross (8)

Harris Primary Academy Haling Park, Croydon

Winter Wonderland

A teenage boy named Nicholas wandered into the woods with his dog, Cuddles. Nicholas didn't believe in Father Christmas anymore, but he spotted a magical door glistening in the middle of the empty woods. Nicholas honestly thought he was dreaming but he wasn't. He opened the magical door and couldn't believe his eyes. Through the magical door was a stunning winter wonderland full of fresh snow and beautifully decorated Christmas trees. As the wind blew, he heard jingle bells behind him, he turned around to be greeted by Father Christmas himself. From that day on Nicholas believed in Father Christmas.

Reuben Hartley-Lewis (11)
Lower Darwen Primary School, Lower Darwen

The Sirens

As darkness overtook light a struggling James Fobom was sipping his glass of wine. As his eyes rested and as sleep started to slowly overtake him. Blaring, purge-like sirens blasted. He decided to follow the noise. He was led to a magical forest. He travelled further in until he was lost. Bright colours clouded his judgement. He stayed there for months and slowly became... unhinged. Familiar sirens rang so he followed them. As he was sprinting the paradise disappeared. He screamed, "Take me back!"
Ten years later he was chasing someone. As he caught up to him sirens blasted.

George Hollings (11)
Lower Darwen Primary School, Lower Darwen

The Mysterious World

As I was walking into the horrific woods I came to a mysterious, wondrous door. I carelessly yanked the door open and found a wonderful world of wonder. I felt a comforting carpet made of candyfloss and unicorns darting in every direction. All I could hear was the deafening sound of dragons roaring at the top of their horrific voices. I could have sworn I tasted a baguette from Paris. The breathtaking smell smelt like chocolate on a cold evening. As I stepped into the magical world a unicorn caught me.

This for me is a never-ending adventurous, relaxing paradise.

Eva Clarke (10)

Lower Darwen Primary School, Lower Darwen

The Enchanted Tree

One day a little girl was playing hide-and-seek when she stumbled across a huge wardrobe. She twisted the handle and walked through. Behind was a cold, frosty forest. As she gazed around she spotted a glittery tree and quickly ran over to investigate. When she reached the tree it started talking to her. "Hi, I am the wish tree, do you want me to grant you a wish?"
"Yes please," said the girl. She asked for a magical unicorn so the tree told her to walk inside him.
"Okay," said the girl and she was never seen again.

Evie Walton (10)
Lower Darwen Primary School, Lower Darwen

Wander In The Dark

At 8pm Lucy was walking her dog as usual but something wasn't right. As she slowly walked on, a giant cloud of mist appeared upon her. Lucy spotted an unusual black and broken gate made of old rusty iron. She hesitated to walk any further. As she walked on, it started to get mistier and darker. She built up her courage and bravely walked in. She saw a blinking blue light in the sky with glittering clouds and tiny mushroom homes. She heard a quiet whispering voice saying, "Lucy, where have you been? We have been expecting you."

Poppy Gillett (11)

Lower Darwen Primary School, Lower Darwen

Him

You walk into a creepy forest and see a very creepy person called 'Him'. He is very tall, almost half a tree size. He starts walking towards you while humming the Barney 'I love you' song. "What do you want?" you scream.

"You!" he says in a dark voice. He runs at you with incredible speed. Then you wake up and wonder, *was it all a dream?* You go down to get breakfast and then you see him standing at the bottom of your stairs. You run down the stairs and charge at him... but you run through him.

Cayden Parsons (10)
Lower Darwen Primary School, Lower Darwen

The Monster Squirrel

A girl went into the woods and saw a red squirrel. It had the fluffiest tail of any squirrel she had seen. The squirrel went up to her and looked her in the eye. She looked into the squirrel's gorgeous eyes in return. It went over to an oak tree but instead of eating one of the nuts surrounding the tree, it pulled the entire thing out of the ground and swallowed it whole. The girl screamed and ran away as fast as she could. Unfortunately, that wasn't fast enough. The squirrel caught up to the girl and devoured her.

Libby Gudgeon (11)

Lower Darwen Primary School, Lower Darwen

A Walk In A Wood

I took a walk through the woods; it was dark and gloomy until it all went weird. The leaves were glittery and blue and the bark was shiny and pink. The grass was soft and squishy and there were oranges growing on an old, rusty gate. I went closer to the gate and opened it. I saw a lake full of orange lilypads and violet fish swimming around. Further on I saw a huge tiger. I walked towards it and stroked it. Then I saw a mint house to live in forever and ever and lived happily with my tiger.

Mary Wilson (10)

Lower Darwen Primary School, Lower Darwen

A Wander In The Woods

Once upon a time, there lived a girl named Alice. One cold winter's day she went for a walk. Alice saw the woods and went in. It seemed very unusual. She walked deeper and deeper into the woods. It was dark and scary. Then she saw a creature. "Oh, it is a rabbit!"

Then the rabbit said, "Hello."

"Argh!" said Alice. "You can talk!"

"Yes," said Rabbit. "My name is Sid and I love people."

"Good!" said Alice.

"Let's go to my house," said Rabbit.

"Okay," said Alice.

"Do you want cookies?"

"Yes please," and they became friends.

Millie Dye (8)

Place Farm Primary Academy, Haverhill

Wander In The Woods

One sunny Sunday morning, there was a group of elves dancing in Woopy Woods, they were celebrating Scarlett's sixth birthday. The elves were feeling ever so jolly and cheerful. Suddenly they saw a shadow moving in the woods. All the elves were worried because they had never seen a monster before. The monster silently entered the woods and Scarlett spoke to him. "Are you hungry?" she asked him.

"I am starving!" cried the monster.

Scarlett showed the monster to the delicious birthday feast and all the elves and the monster danced happily together in Woopy Woods until the sun set.

Ruby Farrant (6)

Place Farm Primary Academy, Haverhill

In The Woods

In the woods, I hear the birds tweeting and squirrels eating nuts. I walk over to the family of squirrels and say, "Hello, my name is Dorothy, what are your names?"
One squirrel squeaks, "Joe, Elizabear, Santa and Doughnut."
We then find a palace together in the woods. Inside the palace is a magnificent ball with lots of people wearing beautiful dresses. The king and queen then tell us, "You have to leave the ball before the squirrels eat all of the food!"
Then the squirrels take me to their tree palace where we find unlimited chocolate nuts. Yum!

Dorothy Kokodinskij
Place Farm Primary Academy, Haverhill

A Walk In The Woods

Once upon a time, there was a girl with beautiful blonde hair called Emily. She was in a lovely house. She went to look in the mirror and fell in the mirror then ended up in the woods. She went for a walk and on her journey, she found a unicorn. The unicorn said, "Well hello there, what's your name?"
"Er... Emily."
"Lovely name," said the unicorn. "Over there is my friend Pugicorn."
"I will go meet her now," said Emily.
"Okay," said the unicorn.
"Hi," said Pugicorn. "Nice dress."

Lillie Whiting (7)
Place Farm Primary Academy, Haverhill

A Wander In The Woods

One evening the twins were sleeping. Then, when the alarm rang they were in a wood. "Where are we?" said the twins.

"Wow, is that a rainbow, tiny unicorn? Let's explore!" So they went exploring.

"Hello there," came a voice.

It was magical. They both felt exhilarated and smelt home. They found an axe and took it with them in case. Suddenly an angry tree didn't let them pass so they began a battle. They had no weapons so they used the axe. They chopped the ugly, annoying tree down. They ran home like lightning. They were happy.

Rodrigo Goncalves (8)

Place Farm Primary Academy, Haverhill

A Wander In The Woods

As Charlotte and her friends stepped into the deep, dark woods they found that they might not be the only ones there. As they trekked through the forest Scarlett noticed something behind the trees. "It's a temple!" shouted Brandon. "Can we stay in it for the night?"
They all agreed as they wanted to get out of the hail that was as hard as bullets and they were as cold as if they'd been walking in the freezing Arctic. They ran into the destroyed temple. Charlotte lit a torch and they all saw two black eyes staring right at them...

Amelia Ives (9)

Place Farm Primary Academy, Haverhill

Following The Rainbow

Once a little girl called Lilah and her older brothers called James and Mikel were bored and went outside to play but suddenly came a storm of bright and colourful raindrops. They slowly swirling around them and made a bright and shimmering pathway through the garden. They followed the pathway which led to the forest, they were worried because they didn't know what was in there. As they looked into the tall trees Lilah pointed to a mysterious creature, all brown and hairy. It roared and they all got scared and ran home to their mother for their roast dinner.

Leah Tomlinson (6)
Place Farm Primary Academy, Haverhill

Wander In The Woods

The time was 2:49am and Holly lay wide awake in her bed. Suddenly she heard a soft, subtle sound. Should Holly investigate? The sound was drifting from the woods. Quietly she tiptoed to the back door. Cautiously she opened the tall, wooden and creaky door. Her family were sound asleep, as was everyone else in the village of Howerton. Howerton Woods sat right behind her house. Feeling very scared, Holly entered the woods. The noise that called to her was now ear-piercing and sounded like bells. Just then Holly saw what it was. What caught her eyes shocked her...

Ellie Farrant (8)

Place Farm Primary Academy, Haverhill

A Wander Through The Woods

There was a girl called Ella. She was walking home when she fell through an open drain but surprisingly it led her to a wood but not an ordinary wood, a magical wood, with fairies, witches, good and bad. "We need your help," a fairy said to Ella. "The bad witch is coming and she's going to destroy the wood. Look!" shouted the fairy. "Here she comes!"

The witch appeared. Everyone was scared as she began to cast a spell to destroy the wood. Ella got out her mirror and reflected the spell back on the witch. She was dead.

Eloise Carpenter (8)

Place Farm Primary Academy, Haverhill

The Lost Girl

Once upon a time, a little girl called Lilly found a fisherman. The fisherman said, "Don't go out to sea, a dangerous creature is going round!"
Lilly didn't listen and hopped onto her mum's boat and went out to sea. The next day Lilly found the creature. It was a killer whale but she fell out of the boat and landed on top of the creature. She said, "What! You are good, you're not dangerous, you are nice!"
That night they were sitting underwater. They thought they should celebrate so they celebrated all night.

Freya Cage (8)
Place Farm Primary Academy, Haverhill

Wander In The Woods

Tommy was in bed when he saw a light. As soon as he touched the light, he vanished into the woods. He saw a witch so he said, "Hi." The witch noticed him but little did Tommy know... she was evil and put a spell on him.

Later a fox came and said, "Be careful! I will unfreeze you!" so he did.

Tommy said, "Thank you."

The fox said, "You're welcome."

Tommy said, "I had better go home."

The fox said, "Okay."

Tommy said, "Okay, goodbye!" to the fox.

Ingrid Dos Reis (8)
Place Farm Primary Academy, Haverhill

Lacey Polarcorn

One day, there was a polarcorn called Lacey, she lived in a castle with her mum and dad. She had a rainbow horn and her wings were rainbow feathers. Every time she flew she would spread glitter everywhere in her town. It made everyone happy in the kingdom.

One day, while she was flying around she saw another polarcorn and they fell in love. His name was Lucas. He had blue and green feathers with a yellow horn.

Two years later, they got married and had twin baby polarcorns and they all lived happily ever after in the magical kingdom.

Lilly Richardson (11)

Place Farm Primary Academy, Haverhill

A Wander In The Woods

Lexi lent down brushing crisp snow off a fallen tree, she was exhausted and needed to sit down to catch her breath. The first snow day of winter, her favourite time of year. Suddenly, she heard a rustling in the trees above, looking up Lexi saw an elf sobbing. The elf explained he was planning a cheeky trick on his family when unexpectedly a crow scooped him up. Lexi told him she had an elf but he could come and join their family too. Happily, they continued wandering through the woods back home and had a very merry Christmas together.

Tiaamii Estall (9)

Place Farm Primary Academy, Haverhill

The Forest Portal

One damp, dark night a boy named Santa Claus ate a fortune cookie. One cookie teleported him to a forest, but not just any forest, the Forbidden Forest of Doom. He was scared of it because he'd heard that most people died who went there! So he was careful. After a while, he found a portal. He went through the portal and found an Animagus which was hiding a glorious bright red crystal from Santa Claus! Santa needed the crystal to be able to escape the Forbidden Forest. Would Santa get back out in time for his elves?

Logan Roberts (8)

Place Farm Primary Academy, Haverhill

A Wander In The Woods

Once upon a time in the scary woods, a little boy waited by a gate, also, he wouldn't go through unless he had a lantern. So he searched around and behind a tree he found what he thought was a light source, which it was. He took it and entered the dark, scary woods. To his surprise, the dark forest wasn't as scary as it had been in there before that day. When he walked further in, he realised he didn't need his lantern anymore since the sun was beaming through the forest. Then he realised it was a dream.

Raymond Walker (8)

Place Farm Primary Academy, Haverhill

A Wander In The Wood

One day, there was a kid named Molly. She was a kind, beautiful, loving girl and loved to have her morning walk at exactly 7am. If not then she would get up and get her coat on and gloves, wellies and a scarf. Then she would get up and go. When she got to the woods she kicked the tree. The tall tree made a sudden move. She stepped back in terror. It was definitely moving. She started running. When she got home she ran straight to bed.

Morning came and she ran back to the wood. It was snowing!

Edie Bee (9)

Place Farm Primary Academy, Haverhill

A Wander In The Woods

Once upon a day, in a small cottage, lived Lana and her caring parents. Around the cottage was a mystical woods. Lana was forbidden to enter the woods but didn't know why. Lana mischievously on the night of her 18th birthday snuck into the woods. As Lana nervously entered the woods she felt the magic. The deeper into it she went, the further back in time she went. Lana saw flashes of her life but suddenly fell and hit her head on a branch.
She woke up in her bed thinking it was all a dream.

Sophia Tooth (9)
Place Farm Primary Academy, Haverhill

A Wander In The Woods

Once upon a time, there was a girl called Ava. She was walking in the woods. Inside the woods she saw a shiny tree. She touched the tree and she saw something drop on the floor. It was a globe. She picked it up and then she turned into a mermaid. She felt happy and jolly. Then the globe opened and she went inside it. She saw glitter and a red stripy starfish. She asked the starfish, "How do you take me back to the woods?" She pushed the globe again and then she was back at the magic tree.

Alexa McBrien (5)

Place Farm Primary Academy, Haverhill

A Wander In The Woods

There once was a little girl that lived in a big castle in a faraway land. She was lying on her bed whilst looking out the window when she saw in the distance a red fox dressed in a fancy yellow suit, walking towards her. As he came closer to the castle he suddenly disappeared down a big hole behind an apple tree. The little girl followed the fox down the hole and found herself in a magical world where foxes ruled the world. She was scared of what she had seen and ran all the way home screaming.

Isabelle Thorncroft (7)
Place Farm Primary Academy, Haverhill

Mission For Berries

One day, I went to the woods to pick berries. Unfortunately, as I went deeper I was getting tired and still there were no berries. Suddenly there was rustling in the bushes. I went to find out what it was. There were cute little creatures with leaves on their heads. I was stunned. I named them Pikmin. They had the power to mind-read as they gave me berries. I told them to follow me if they wanted to be my pets. When I got home we were all partying. Mum baked us all a lovely, yummy berry cake.

Adam Drozd
Place Farm Primary Academy, Haverhill

A Wander In The Woods

Once upon a time, there was a door with wonder...
A little girl went into a forest. The girl was called
Lucy. She found a mysterious door but Lucy was
too scared to go through the door. The next day
Lucy went back to the forest and she went through
the door. *Boom! Bang!* Into the magical land.
"Argh! Someone, help me! Hi, who are you?"
"I'm visible but not in the dark. I will see you in
your dreams when you go home and go to sleep
then you will see me."

Harvey Barros (8)

Place Farm Primary Academy, Haverhill

A Wander In The Woods

Once upon a time, a girl was sleeping then she woke up. She saw a magical wood. In the woods, she saw a unicorn. It was dark now, she was going to explore the woods. She did not find anything, she kept on trying but she still didn't find anything. She carried on walking through the woods. She did find a cocoon but she didn't need it. She kept walking. She still walked. She felt exhilarated and tired. She wanted to have a break. She ran to her house and lived happily ever after.

Charlotte Goncalves (5)
Place Farm Primary Academy, Haverhill

Wander In The Woods

One hot day a girl called Poppy went for a picnic in the woods with her dad. Dad went to sleep so Poppy went for a wander and bumped right into a squirrel looking for nuts. Poppy knew Dad had nuts in his picnic so she went to get some. Squirrel enjoyed the nuts and ate them all up quickly but he saved a few for Mrs Squirrel and off he went to take her them. Dad woke up just as Squirrel left. He was hungry so had a sandwich and looked for the nuts but they weren't there anymore!

Poppy Sorrell (7)

Place Farm Primary Academy, Haverhill

My Discovery In The Wood

One day, I was walking calmly in the woods of golden magic at sunset. The trees of golden light were making such big shadows that the forest felt dark, damp and dangerous. When I heard a sound, I was extremely scared but then I realised it was only a baby wolf. I wanted to keep him so he accepted straight away. We went home, chattering away. My house was in the middle of the woods. We slept there and in the morning we went hunting in the wonderful woods, then we came home safely.

Elena Chodorge (8)

Place Farm Primary Academy, Haverhill

A Wander In The Woods

Once upon a time there lived a girl and a boy. Their names were Rosey and Tom. Rosey was from a village and Tom was from a forest. Tom wanted to discover the world so he did. When he was halfway around the world he was in a village. He met a girl who was as pretty as a butterfly. The girl was as thin as a pencil. He said to her, "Let's go for a stroll in the woods." They went on and on, it was like the time was going slowly. The time was like slow motion...

Ruby Mason (7)
Place Farm Primary Academy, Haverhill

Wander In The Woods

Once upon a time, there was an eight-year-old boy called Tim and Tim was outside the woods. He felt terrified then he went in the woods. It was dark and scary. It smelt like a unicorn was coming. Tim saw the unicorn, it was colourful and sparkly and smelt like sweets. Tim climbed on the unicorn and went for a ride through the woods. He climbed on the trees and found a magical gem. It was very sparkly! Then he heard his mum calling but he could not find his way back.

Samuel Leahy

Place Farm Primary Academy, Haverhill

A Wander In The Woods

One day a person was having a wander in the woods. Then he heard a noise. "What is that noise?" he said. He continued to walk. Then it became night and he went to sleep in his tent. "Morning time!" he shouted. Then he got out of his tent. All of a sudden a monkey dropped and took his hat and bananas! He ran after the monkey but he ran out of breath so he went back to his tent to get his lunch then he started relaxing and he lived happily after.

Danny Colman (7)
Place Farm Primary Academy, Haverhill

A Wander In The Woods

I was wandering in the woods on a very sunny day with my daddy, Claire and my brothers Scott and Ollie when I saw an owl in a tree. He told me that the woods were magical and I could have three wishes. I wished for a sunny holiday with a huge swimming pool, a new Lego set and fishing every weekend with my daddy. The owl told me that he would give me all my wishes and it made me very happy. The walk in the woods to meet the owl was my favourite day ever.

James Langley
Place Farm Primary Academy, Haverhill

My Dog Dennis

My mum and I have a dog, our dog's name is Dennis. He is brown and has a little brown stripe on his back. Dennis likes to play with me and my mum. He can jump and run fast. Dennis likes to play with his friend Alfie. Alfie is a very fat dog. Dennis and Alfie run in the hot sun, they dig in the mud. Dennis and Alfie run by a cat. The cat does not like the dogs, she likes to sleep on her bed. My mum and I love our cat Rogue and our dog called Dennis.

Lilly Smith (10)

Place Farm Primary Academy, Haverhill

The Three Friends

One time there were three friends called Filip, Edi and Tyler. They found a rock and the rock gave all of them one wish. The wish that all of them chose was a superpower. Edi got really fast. Tyler had electricity in his hands and Filip could fly. They all became superheroes. They were known as the friends who found a rock and turned into superheroes.

Filip Togaczynski (8)
Place Farm Primary Academy, Haverhill

A Wander In The Woods

In the forest I play with my sister. There are leaves in the forest and twigs and sticks and trees. We shake the trees and the leaves come off.
We love playing in the forest. We find some animals like foxes and squirrels. We find moles in the forest and we find some leaves in the forest.

Daisy Darvill (6)

Place Farm Primary Academy, Haverhill

A Wander In The Woods

"Aaaahh!" Jane and Shaun woke up next to a tree.

"W-where are we?" shouted Jane.

"I-I don't know," said Shaun.

"Oh, I remember, we fell off a cliff and we are in a misty forest," said Jane.

"Oh, I remember now, why are the mushrooms so big?"

"I don't know."

The trees, they're all pine trees," said Shaun.

Thump, thump, thump!

"What was that?"

Thump, thump, thump!

"There's a mushroom monster!" shrieked Jane.

"Run!"

"Mushy, mooshy," said the monster.

"We're cornered."

"I'll help you," said the monster.

He turned into a ladder and they went home.

Alf Orford (10)

Ripley Court School, Ripley

Stop The Chop!

"Stop!" I cried. They couldn't destroy the woods. It was the animals' home. I sprinted to the edge of the woods where the grating noise of the machinery was coming from. When I got there they had only cut down one tree, for now! *Crash!* Another went down. "Stop!" I yelled.

A man said, "You don't want to get involved!"

"But I already am!"

"Go away!" he replied.

"No, this is my home. You can't destroy a human's habitat," I shouted coldly.

"Oh no," he shouted to his mates, "she is right."

Once they left I wandered in the woods.

Evelyn Shaw (10)

Ripley Court School, Ripley

God Goes On A Walk

Today God went on a walk in the forest. "This is so nice! I should come here again," said God.
"You dare enter my forest, out!" screamed a roaring voice.
"You see... I'm God and this is my property... technically."
"Get out!"
As a massive scary figure rose out the ground all God could say was, "Oh... you're approaching me? I built this whole place and you!"
"Get out!"
"Look, I don't want to kill you... but I will throw you in an infinite loop of spinning."
God then threw him into an infinite loop of spinning. "Peace, finally."

Aiden Tyack-Hamadi (10)

Ripley Court School, Ripley

Little Road

I woke up in a strange place with a faint taste of chocolate in my mouth. There was a tiny square of a leaf. I then realised where I was. There was a sign that said *Little Road*.

"What's that?" a small voice said. "It's a giant, run!"

I looked down to see tiny people. "Wait, I'm not a giant, I'm a human."

The little people stopped.

"Can I help you?"

"Yes please by getting us food. We gnomes are starving. We need help."

"What do you gnomes eat?"

"We eat wood, wood is everywhere."

I got wood for them.

Thomas Caine (10)
Ripley Court School, Ripley

Living In The Woods

"Argh!" cried Nancy, swinging on the tree branches going branch to branch. "There's a gorilla chasing me!" She stopped high up a tree where the gorilla couldn't get her. The gorilla tried to climb up the tree after Nancy. Nancy jumped off her branch into the next tree, leaving the gorilla behind. The gorilla tried again to catch Nancy but Nancy just laughed. It was Nancy's gorilla friend chasing her – they were playing 'it'! Then it was time for tea so Nancy and the gorilla went inside and had delicious pumpkin pie and vegetables. A fun day in the woods!

Nancy O'Rourke (9)

Ripley Court School, Ripley

A Wander In The Woods

Ding went my alarm clock. Time to walk my dog so I walked my dog in the woods. I saw a hole in a tree. It was quite strange because a single sound was coming from the tree hole.

"Hello, my name is Bob," he said in a jolly way.

"Who are you?" I said.

Straight away he said he was an elf.

"What?! You can't be an elf. Well, if you are, build something with this fallen tree," I said strongly.

Crrrr, bang!

"Done!" Bob said.

"Wow, I believe you now. Goodbye, Bob."

"Bye," Bob whispered.

Ayesha Nagelson (10)

Ripley Court School, Ripley

Minotaur

"Come on, Harry!" shouted Tristan.

"Coming!" I groaned, climbing over a fallen tree.

When I reached Tristan he was inspecting a bush.

"Hmm," Tristan said.

I must mention that we are demigods on a quest to kill the Minotaur.

"What's wrong?" I asked.

The bush rustled, out came the Minotaur... He was ripped, short hair all over. Before I could unsheath my sword he charged! I jumped out of the way.

Crack! The Minotaur hit a tree so hard it fell over - his horns stuck in the tree. Tristan and I attacked. The Minotaur was dead.

Harry Goggin (10)

Ripley Court School, Ripley

Those Five Hours

Zap! Sophie was out cold. She found herself sitting on a swing. Sophie recognised it, she was in the same wood she was in before, but it was different. *The fungi, that's what it was,* thought Sophie. "When it zapped me it transported me here! I might as well enjoy myself," she exclaimed happily. She danced in a ring of roses, daisies, foxbells and willow. All of a sudden she thought something, *I'm stuck here!* She ran to the swing and swung really high. She was back and couldn't remember anything that had happened to her in those five hours!

Naina Sharma (10)

Ripley Court School, Ripley

The Ancient Adventure

"Argh!" came the cries of the trees.

"Hiss!" came the whispers of the leaves.

I looked behind myself and saw something gigantic emerging. It started running towards me becoming clearer and clearer every second. Then everything went black.

The next day, though it felt longer, I woke up in a wood surrounded by strange people. I sat up and found I was sitting on a bed of leaves. I jumped down from the multicoloured beanbag and looked around. I saw a small package of nut shells and immediately realised it was pixies. All sorts of different colours.

Juliana Lima (9)

Ripley Court School, Ripley

A Wander In The Woods

Grace was dancing in the leaves when the tree fell. It revealed a baby horse with a white mane and tail. It jumped up at Grace. She screamed and backed away. The horse came towards her again as if it wanted to be her friend. "Hello! You're so cute. I'm going to name you, hmm, Rosie!"
Ten minutes later, Grace came back with food. Rosie ate it all up in seconds, then galloped through the woods, past Grace, thankful for her food. *Where are Rosie's parents?* Grace wondered. Rosie was happy. Grace and Rosie galloped through the sunny woods together.

Sophie Pascoe (10)
Ripley Court School, Ripley

The Lost School

"Hello, is anyone there?" I cried. We were on a camping trip and everyone had disappeared. All I could hear were the birds singing and trees rustling. As I stepped forward I felt the ground squelching under my feet. I was so confused, so alone. I ran quickly, trying to reach help, but the woods just kept on going. I was beginning to think that I'd disappeared. "Can someone help?" I shouted. Just then I saw something out of the corner of my eye. I stepped over the twisting tree which was infested with glowing fungi.
I'd found a school.

Katie Mathur (9)
Ripley Court School, Ripley

The Case

Anxiously, Charlie sat in his lesson, someone was hiding something. Next to him was James, the new boy. His pencil case was a mechanical one with lots of buttons. Charlie's hand was hovering above the case. In shock, his hand tapped the case. At the speed of light, Charlie was sucked into the case, into a dark abyss. Charlie fell far for a little boy. A gargantuan splash filled the room. James was shocked! The splash led to Charlie swimming in a pool.

Five minutes later he arrived back in a soggy classroom. Everyone was shocked and wet. "Wow!"

James Collins (10)

Ripley Court School, Ripley

The Way Home

It was a dark evening and Lily was lost in the woods. *What was that?* Lily thought to herself. She went to explore! After a while of looking she saw something in the leaves, there it was, a fluffy, blue thing. It looked like a rabbit crossed with a fox. There was a fallen tree and the roots looked like a waterfall. The rabbit fox said, "Hello, I am Blueberry."

Lily replied, "Hello, I am Lily."

After a while, they became friends. An hour later Lily went up her driveway. Blueberry looked sad. They never saw each other again.

Jasmin Knight (10)

Ripley Court School, Ripley

A Whole New World

An ominous silhouette of a man shocked me to the bone. There were more like him standing pale-faced. I wandered over to them. Each man was standing in front of a tree. One grabbed me by the arm. "You're coming with me."
We were walking very fast. I loosened his grip and ran to a pond. I submerged myself and waited. I was falling through the water and ended up in a forest with sable trees, turquoise wood and grass soft like silk. The man who dragged me appeared and was carried away.
"Yes I'm free, I'll never leave."

James Bevan (10)
Ripley Court School, Ripley

The Lost Girl

I woke up on my bed of leaves scared of my dream. I then saw the girl. I don't know how she got here. I quickly got into my furs. Later I asked her, "Who are you?"

"Sarah!"

"Hi Sarah, I'm Jerald," I replied, "and I live in the woods."

A piece of paper fell out of her pocket, it had an address on it - The Woodland Lodge.

"Let's get you home."

After I returned Sarah home her family bought the woods and gave me the land. Every now and again I go for a wander in the woods.

James Batten (9)
Ripley Court School, Ripley

Winter

Everything is dead! I hate winter and all the death it brings. All the trees are dead and are left without any leaves. Even the animals are dead and they are usually the liveliest things about forests. Nothing living in sight. Snow covers the forest like a large white blanket. A small flower is just poking up through the ground. *Thud!* It gets covered by thick snow. It's dead! Winter is the worst, it brings malign snow, Jack Frost and hurtling winds. I cannot wait for joy-taking winter to go! Spring will you come soon? Winter's killing!

Matilda Coen (10)
Ripley Court School, Ripley

A Wander In The Woods

There was darkness everywhere. I didn't know where I was and then, all of a sudden, I was in an enchanted wood. I was surrounded by blue trees. A purple roof made from the leaves of them. I looked around, questions filling my head. After a while of walking I saw a mushroom house. I felt the urge to go inside and look around. When I arrived at the mushroom house I knocked on the door. "Come in!" said a quiet voice. I opened the door and saw... "Do your homework," shouted my mum.
That was a very nice daydream!

Alexandra Mann (10)
Ripley Court School, Ripley

A Wander In The Woods

"I will always regret this. I am in a big windy wood with nobody around." What could I do? I could run and say to my parents I couldn't survive the night or just be brave. "Um? I will be brave. But wait a minute, what's that? I think it is a blue and red tree but this is an oak forest." I went up a bit closer and more appeared! "The trees are towering over me, they're surrounding me. Help!"
One hour later I was camping out under the only tree left. I had survived but desperately needed help.

Daniel Gillam (10)
Ripley Court School, Ripley

A Dragon's Shadow

Wolves howled as the sun faded in the distance. Out my window I saw a dragon's shadow in a storm cloud. *Bang!* A bolt of lightning hit the dragon...

The next day I went for a wander in the woods, I found a fifty-foot long dragon skeleton. I thought I was going crazy but there was a unicorn behind the gigantic, tall pine tree. It stared at me and *bang!* Another strike of lightning set the forest on fire. After that I needed to sprint out of the forest. Maybe that is why I heard some terrified wolves howling...

Leo Necmi (9)

Ripley Court School, Ripley

The Wander In The Woods

I'm alone in the world. The only thing keeping me company, the woods. One day I wandered in. I don't know if it was fate, but I tripped and my ear pressed against a tree. I was hearing strange words, "You were born here, the daughter of the king and queen tree."
Next I heard the same words coming from the surrounding trees. Golden leaves fell into a path. I followed them, finally seeing two glistening oaks. I knew I had to bow. The trees told me to be a warrior and help the trees. My fate became clear finally.

Callista Cumberland (11)
Ripley Court School, Ripley

A Wander In The Woods

I woke up on an uncomfortable bed and looked into the darkness of my tent. I went to a camp but so far it had been boring. It was midnight and I scrambled out my tent and started to walk. The camp was next to some woods so I wandered into them. It was full of crunchy leaves and gargantuan trees. I was so amazed that I stopped concentrating and tripped. The next thing I knew was that the camp manager was shouting, "You should never have gone into the woods! You're banned from camp!"
I left, flooded with despair.

Alice Nash (10)
Ripley Court School, Ripley

The Crystal Woods

The twisted gate opened, revealing a crystal forest. I stepped inside. At the end of the forest a purple tree arose. I ran, I was desperate to see it. The leaves swirled behind me, I realised there was a pink unicorn. It galloped past me to the purple tree. I followed, curious to see where it was going. We finally got to the purple tree. When the unicorn jumped up onto the tree it shattered to pieces. The pieces grouped together to make a sentence, 'I will grant any wish'. I wished to live in these magical woods forever.

Sophia Smith (10)
Ripley Court School, Ripley

A Wander In The Woods

Suddenly I heard the gate open so I walked through. Immediately I felt myself falling. I expected the landing to hurt, but it didn't. Suddenly, I heard a roar. I looked behind me, the gate had vanished. I was trapped in the woods! The roar was a dragon. I knew it, even if I couldn't see it through the woods. It would kill me. Suddenly a unicorn appeared and attacked the dragon, it died. I ran towards where the unicorn had been. All there was was the gate. I ran quickly towards the gate. As I walked through I transported.

Arthur Ogilive Smals (10)
Ripley Court School, Ripley

A Wander In The Woods

Lost, I stumbled into a mountain of autumn leaves. Where was I? A wave of darkness surrounded me. I stood and looked around. Warily, I walked on. It was getting lighter. The trees were rough and bumpy, lines cracked through. In one tree I could hear humming. I looked up and could not believe my eyes. It was a beautiful hummingbird. It flew round my head, singing at me like it wanted me to follow. I followed the incredible bird into an empty clearing and then I saw my wonderful family. I ran towards them and hugged them tightly.

Lara Bailey (10)
Ripley Court School, Ripley

The Woods

In the woods a pine tree, different from the others, was surrounded by vines. It had a tint. The tree was guarding something. People went into it and never came out. Something was wrong about it, it had a sign. I've heard that the sign said... *Where is the cave? The treasure's inside. You may never know...* or something along those lines. I wanted to go. I packed and set off. The entrance was huge. I entered. It was a drowsy place, I felt sleepier and sleepier. Darkness surrounded me, I fell to the hard floor...

Ella Kemp (10)
Ripley Court School, Ripley

The Wonderful Woods

As I walk through the thick, dark woods I listen to the birds high up in the trees, singing like nobody is listening. I can hear the rustling in the leaves where the rabbits hop. I can feel the strong gusts of wind blowing through my hair. I can see the squirrels gnawing on the starchy centres of the walnuts. The clouds are opening up above and letting beautiful rays of sunshine seep through the gaps. The leaves are floating down from the trees as if they are defying gravity. I can taste the sweet thin air hovering around me.

Max Lippiett (10)
Ripley Court School, Ripley

The Enchanted Magical Woods

Once upon a time a girl called Millie flew to the top of the trees. She could see leaves as orange as a tiger and heard crunches echoing like a branch snapping. Millie could hear unicorns, dragons and little fairies or elves crying. The woods were absolutely colossal. Millie flew down to find a little fairy, her eyes were red and had a sparkling glow that seemed to trap her. Millie is the Queen of the Forest. A boy trapped her by surprise, his name was Drogo. He was killed by Millie and Millie can rule the wood once again.

Emilie Dick (9)

Ripley Court School, Ripley

Lost In The Woods

"Where are you?" I called. "Hello?" I was on a family walk in the woods and we'd just had our picnic. I'd left my bag behind so I'd gone to get it but there was no sign of my family. I walked through the woods shouting, "Hello?" Leaves were blowing around all the beech trees. Suddenly I noticed there was one random oak tree in the middle of all the beech trees. I was about to walk away but my name was carved into it! I reached out to touch it and *bang!* I was back at home!

Sophie Stephens (10)

Ripley Court School, Ripley

The Fallen Tree

Swoosh! The tree fell into the lake. All the animals drinking from the lake fled to safe ground. At this point Alexa was sprinting to the lake to see what happened. "Oh no, what happened? It looks as if the tree has fallen and now all the deer can't drink and the next forest is miles away. Looks like I will have to find another lake for them," debated Alexa. Alexa walked around trying to find a new lake for the animals and when she found a new lake she made sure that the animals knew where it was.

Iris Watt (9)
Ripley Court School, Ripley

The Girl, The Fox And Me

"Stop, stop!" Two men were dragging me somewhere, another man opened two black gates. I screamed, they dropped me. I was in a dark wood. I saw a fox, it was beautiful. I walked up to it. It turned into a little girl.
The girl said, "You're in the enchanted wood, follow me."
The girl went up a tree, I tried to follow but was taken up by a cloud. There were lots of tiny doors built into the tree. I looked down at the wood. I fell but the cloud caught me. The girl changed back into a fox.

Isabel Forwood (9)
Ripley Court School, Ripley

A Wander In The Woods

It changed my life when I stepped into the woods earlier that day. I was frozen with fear, I had seen something leaping into the shadows of the trees. I followed it into the woods until I came across a mysterious-looking tree. I knew it wasn't a normal tree, it was rigid, unique and different. It had no leaves but was definitely alive. The branches were wriggly and curly like ivy vines but I spotted a lonely leaf sitting upon the tree. I went around the tree until I came across a hole. I went in and found secrets.

Martha Wilcockson (10)
Ripley Court School, Ripley

Dark Windy Woods

I have lost everything, my parents, my brother, just alone in these dark, cold woods thinking about all the happiness I had. Wind blowing through my hair, leaves falling on me. Hi, my name is Jake. I'm pretty skinny, long blond hair and very shy because I have not talked to anyone. I get up, wipe my golden, shiny tears off my face and then explore the place. I walk on hearing noises in my head. I approach the place with trees with weird markings on them, the swamp near me, gives me a wish to see my parents again.

Jack Sparks (10)
Ripley Court School, Ripley

A Wander In The Woods

On the hill was a forbidden forest but I was curious. I went to the old forest gate, kicked it open with an easy push. I headed on through the dark, gloomy forest. Weeds grew freely in the forest. One berry hung in front of me. I knew I shouldn't but I ate it. Suddenly my surroundings changed into a mythical world. The weeds sprouted up into multicoloured trees and birds changed to flaming dragons. I took a moment but a dragon turned to me and growled. I ate another berry and went back. I am not going back again.

Oliver Tiernan (10)

Ripley Court School, Ripley

The Wander In The Woods

I woke up on the canopy of the Amazon rainforest. Suddenly I slipped and fell. I must have passed out because now I was on the forest floor with a sloth licking my face. I got away then looked down at my body. My clothes were ripped, I was scratched to death. I had to get water. Fortunately, it was rainy season so I had plenty of that but did have to get somewhere before the wildlife hungrily came out. Unfortunately, I had nothing to protect myself. Finally, I found signs pointing to a place called Rio de Janeiro...

Oscar Gill (10)
Ripley Court School, Ripley

A Wander In The Woods

Tim was frustrated, it was that same tree again. This was the third time he had seen it. He was lost. He looked up at the green coverage. He screamed loudly. He looked forward and walked. He saw a shining tree in the darkness. *Just the light*, he thought. He thought that he saw a dog but now he was seeing things. But then he heard a whining and out came a dog. Tim smiled, he always wanted a dog. "Here boy," he said calmly. He was holding something in his mouth. A map! They were going to be friends.

Tom Douthett (10)
Ripley Court School, Ripley

A Wander In The Woods

We've ruined the world! I look around. Yes, I am in the woods which is nature. Yes, the woods are my favourite place to be... but look at it. Walking around I hear sweet chirping from the birds and the rustle of autumn leaves but... something is wrong. I can smell chemicals, different types. It is a melancholy place. The repugnant smells are the type that you can smell in a factory. Nature is beautiful but out of the corner of my eye vibrant orange litter is on the floor. I pick it up. A tear rolls down my eye.

Poppy Renshaw (10)
Ripley Court School, Ripley

My Hatred Of Forests

I just didn't like it, it felt horrible. The feeling crept through my veins like a slithery snake. This is my sense of something sinister. It all started six months ago when I was on a walk in the woods with my parents. I interested myself in a ladybug until I accidentally killed it. When I got up my parents were gone. My parents must not have noticed me stop. I then noticed it, a wolf, sneaking through the bushes. I tried to run but it attacked me. I hate wolves and to this day, I really, really hate wolves.

Mario Valenta (10)
Ripley Court School, Ripley

A Wander In The Woods

Maya walked through the mysterious gates into an old and uneven garden. She walked through a creepy door. She stood in a damp, warm house. She decided it would not be a suitable place for the night so she went back out the gates. She wandered through the frightful forest. It was muggy. She then saw a small, ragged tent rolled up. She put it up with ease. The night was near so she went to sleep. She woke up uncomfortable but she got up and walked back to the house but it was not there. She gasped in surprise.

Lior Reich (9)
Ripley Court School, Ripley

The Sheep Of Terror

Excited, scared, amazed, I was woken up by a tree falling down. Leaves were falling down like rain from clouds. It was amazing but scary. I thought I was going to have a heart attack. The sound didn't only wake me up but also a man-eating sheep! Its baa was louder than the tree falling down. It trotted over really fast and I had to face it. I picked up a stick of around one metre. It charged but missed. I took a swing with my stick and it missed. I tried again and it luckily hit. I celebrated afterwards.

Alex Maroudas (9)
Ripley Court School, Ripley

The Magical Woods

At midnight I heard the rattle of leaves in the woods opposite my house. I went into the woods and saw a talking leaf. I then saw and heard dragons blowing fire, flying leaves. I saw a very big pond, it was glowing. I went into it, there were pink diamonds, purple, blue, green, red and yellow. There was a rainbow bear and it was chasing me. It fell into a hole and I saw fairies dancing with foxes. "That's very odd!" I then tripped and I was home. When I told my mum she didn't believe me.

Daisy Constable (9)

Ripley Court School, Ripley

The Shadow Vs Light

I saw a glimmer of blinding light through the cracks of the gate. There were trees with crystals for stems and floating water for leaves. On the other side of the forest it was just dark, not magical, the trees were made out of charcoal and the stems were made out of burnt wood. I saw only crows and sparrows. I also saw a dark sorcerer with a crow on his right shoulder, it seemed that when he stepped into the light he would die. I went into the dark and pushed him into the light and saw him disintegrate.

Marius Boyd (10)
Ripley Court School, Ripley

A Wander In The Woods

I tried to enjoy myself but the smell of the trees put me off. I was behind and my mum shouted cacophonously towards me. I hate the woods, the smell and all the animals that live there. I would rather be at home. Suddenly I saw something that caught my eye. I saw a tree, but this wasn't your average bumpy, rigid, grey tree; it was unusual, unique and exquisite. The tree had a hole in it with a bright light. This is a magical tree, no it's a magical forest. The tree is a massive part of my life.

Jorja Asumang (10)

Ripley Court School, Ripley

The Golden Stag

Recently I had the best experience. I was in a wood. The crows cawed above my head. It distracted me from thinking. I was on a tree stump. As I stood up I felt strange. I floated away. I was high up above the towering trees. Seeing a clearing in the trees I floated down to it. There was light coming from it and there stood a magnificent creature, it was a golden stag standing by a splashing waterfall. I reached out to touch it. It was soft and the light was dazzling. I never saw anything like it again.

Alice Knight (9)

Ripley Court School, Ripley

A Wander In The Woods

I often stared longingly over the fence at the magic wood. I liked to come up with fantasies about it. I decided there and then that I would run away and live in the magic wood. I looked behind me to check no one was watching, then jumped over the fence. My socks caught on brambles. I could already hear them calling. I didn't listen. The wood was magic. I ran and danced with fairies until I was in a swamp. An arm was suddenly grabbing me. I had to say goodbye to my wood. One day I'll be back.

Pip Roberts (10)
Ripley Court School, Ripley

The Last Ladybug

In the woods a ladybug awoke with a big worry. The dogs were climbing up the trees. They were getting closer with every breath she took. She did not know what to do but run. She ran for days on end with nowhere to go and nothing to eat but berries. Finally she found a calm, peaceful place in the countryside where she had to build a hut on the outskirts of a small town. She earnt her money in a peaceful barber's shop that is located in the roots of an old fallen over tree in the gorgeous woods.

Sophie Mills (10)
Ripley Court School, Ripley

The Minotaur In The Woods

Once upon a time, there was a wood near the goblin village. At night I decided to go to the wood. All of a sudden, I heard a Minotaur roaring. The goblins heard it and they came rushing out of the village. They struggled to kill it but I shot it in the back of the head. It screamed and fell to the ground. We'd done it we'd killed it. We took all of our strongest goblin men and took the Minotaur to the bonfire and burnt its body. We all had some Minotaur to eat and had loud fireworks.

Poppy Miller (9)
Ripley Court School, Ripley

The Tree

I woke up high in the tree, terrified by the bright lightning. I then slipped, tumbling to the ground but I quickly pulled out my wings at the last second and flew away. Whilst falling I saw a mysterious puddle. I flew down to it to have a drink but when I got to the puddle a crocodile jumped out so I pecked the crocodile. He tried to bite me but I jumped on his head. After many minutes fighting he gave up and I had won the forest forever. The crocodile became my servant. I love being a bird.

Cameron Hermiston (11)

Ripley Court School, Ripley

The Tale From All The Tree Tops

I woke up on a bus travelling to the woods. It was the last stop so I got off there. The woods are an interesting place, oh my name is Jack. The soulless leaves that fell in autumn lay dead on the damp floor. I am a hunter and I arrived here to get some food. I'd already caught some deer, but I wanted more for my family. I spotted blurs of white elegance so I started to chase it. At once it stopped and I saw the dashing horse munching on grass. Quickly I left the woods without stressing.

Benjamin Everitt (9)

Ripley Court School, Ripley

The Tree Trunk

A boy wanders into the woods but finds himself lost in the middle of the woods. Suddenly he hears a rustle in the bushes. He starts running as fast as he can even though he is a brave boy. Then he turns around and finds out it is just a squirrel! He starts to follow the squirrel until the squirrel goes up a tree. The boy makes a ladder out of branches he finds. He climbs into the tree and feeds the squirrel some nuts. After, he finds his way out of the forest to where his Dad is waiting.

Harry O'Gilvie (10)

Ripley Court School, Ripley

Wander In The Woods

I found this weird dark wood. I said, "What is this place?" I went in, not knowing what I might find. Suddenly while I was walking I heard rustles in the bushes. Luckily it was just a squirrel. It was carrying nuts and I looked over. I then spotted a cave full of water. I saw something shiny. I jumped in and grabbed it and it was a shiny gem. I looked up - there was a house. I went up to it and there was a gem-shaped lock and I opened it. Then the cave started to close...

Daniel Peyton (10)
Ripley Court School, Ripley

A Battle In The Woods

I am an elf, a good archer. I woke up and thought, *what am I going to hunt today?* I went hunting. I went to hunt deer. Soon after I left to go hunting I met a dragon, I started shooting arrows like mad. The dragon blew a blast of flames, it burned me. I finally managed to take the dragon down, though I had a big burn on my bow arm. I set out on an adventure to find the healing tree. I found it after getting rid of the guardians. I touched the tree, it healed me.

Nate Eustace (10)
Ripley Court School, Ripley

The Weird Forest

Max and I went into a weird, terrific forest. We found a glowing tree above us, it was creepy. Max and I carried on. We set up a stick den near an edible tree for food and near a waterfall for water. We made a fire and chiselled a toothpick out of wood. Next we made a trap so we could have chicken for dinner on the fire. We went to go and catch a chicken for dinner. "Hooray, we have caught one." We went to sleep after eating the amazing, delicious, juicy fat chicken.

Tyler Engelbrecht (9)

Ripley Court School, Ripley

The Woods

One morning, I went to the dark woods. When I got to the woods, I heard a noise. It was an animal. I wasn't far into the woods. Then I went further and I heard nothing. No noise. Suddenly, I came to a pretty grey horse! The horse started to run towards me. "Argh - run, run!" I yelled. Phew - the horse ran away too. I fell over, which was annoying, but I got up and I was safe. I was lost, but then I saw my tracks. I followed them and made my way out of the woods.

Harry O'Sullivan (9)
Ripley Court School, Ripley

Iris And I

Iris and I went to a new, mysterious place in the woods. A loud noise was coming from the trees. A tree fell down as we ran. Iris said, "Oh no, the animals." We ran and made sure the animals were okay. We found a deer and a baby deer. The mum was hurt from the fall. We took her to shelter with her baby. We fed them the water from our bags and the mum got up slowly. We heard a rustle from the bushes and the mum ran off as if nothing happened. She fled like the wind.

Alexa France (9)
Ripley Court School, Ripley

The Mystery Noise

"Argh, what is that noise?" said John when he was woken up by a noise in the woods. John got out to see what the noise was but there was nothing there. The next day he went to check and he saw bugs in a rotten piece of wood. John cleaned it out then walked out and heard the leaves rustling. He went back home. The next morning when John woke up he saw that all the bugs were in his bed! He screamed as loud as he could, so loud that all the birds flew up in the air!

Tish O'Gilvie (9)
Ripley Court School, Ripley

The Enchanted Forest

I was tumbling, head over toe. A tree root whacked me in the face. I woke up, I had a horrible headache. I tried to move but something was holding me down. I looked down to see what it was, it was a dozen tree roots. I tried to move but they wouldn't budge.

Twenty minutes later I had taken off five roots and now my upper body was free. A root came off my left arm. I breathed a sigh of relief, my left arm undid the right root. I was running and I was free forever!

Toby Holdsworth (11)

Ripley Court School, Ripley

A Wander In The Woods

The gate opened, I walked through. There in front of me were hundreds of fairies. One dainty fairy flew to me and told me to follow her. We walked through the woods. I could hear the wind blowing and the crunch of the leaves. We got to a tree and a door opened. We walked in and sat at a table. She brought out a cake and we sat in silence eating it. She then said her name was Lilia. We chatted for a while, then I fell asleep in my chair. I woke up, it was all a dream.

Jessica Lush (9)
Ripley Court School, Ripley

Campervan

I was lonely in the woods living in a campervan. It was old and broken though inside it was nice with varnished wood. I got water from the stream and cooked on a fire. I slept in the back of it. It was very cosy. I harvested berries and killed deer and sheep. One day the stream froze, it was so bad I had to get an old can and pour embers from my fire in it using sticks. Sadly I took it down to the river and dropped it in and the ice melted. I got water and survived.

Daniel Bimson (9)
Ripley Court School, Ripley

The Woods

I woke up scared in a nightmare. I had heard a noise. It was a bird singing in the woods and the sunrise. I saw a beautiful pond glistening in the sun. It looked like shining diamonds. I saw a fallen-down tree, the roots were tied up and it was the end for that tree. I saw one tree which was naked, all the leaves had fallen off and more were growing. I took a wander round and I saw a gate in a wooden fence. I opened it. I saw my dad standing there, waiting for me.

Alfie Rice (10)
Ripley Court School, Ripley

A Magical, Wondrous Dragon

Once upon a time trees could move all around, birds were tweeting and I was so scared. I saw a beech tree with my name on it. I was surprised. Something flew around it. It was a magical, wondrous walk in the woods. I wondered if I could call a dragon. I whistled and a dragon came. I got on and I rode it to a magical cave, it was amazing. I was never going back home, it was too amazing, the food, the animals, the houses, the beds, the seafood and everything else.

Amy French (9)
Ripley Court School, Ripley

Ready To Fly

I arrived at the woods ready to fly. I switched into first gear and off I went. As I went down the hill twisting and turning, drifting and jumping there was an upcoming jump, a huge jump. I put my foot down on the run-up. I got so much speed that I managed to do a backflip. As I went round everything was a blur. I managed to land, not a very soft one. I was sliding everywhere. Racing down I saw the end of the track and I did an amazing sliding drift to finish.

Charlie Carr (11)

Ripley Court School, Ripley

A Wander In The Forest

I woke up in an old, dented tree. I slowly opened my eyes. I was in a forest. I heard the leaves rustling. What was it? I saw a bear! I ran for my life and I saw a tree. I decided to climb it. I got up and the bear climbed up. I had to jump down. I saw a shed and climbed in. I was finally safe. The bear was trying to get in. I saw a way out so quickly snuck out and the big, scary bear didn't even notice. I got home happy to be alive.

Max Ground (10)
Ripley Court School, Ripley

Nightmare

Running through the woods, Sam and Josh wondered what Mum had meant when she said you might meet something. As the sky darkened and it started to rain, the brothers heard a wolf howling in the distance. Suddenly, their torches flickered off and Sam thought he saw Josh being dragged into a bush. Trying to escape the haunted woods, Sam found a moonlit clearing. Squinting into the darkness, he could see a hooded figure leaning over Josh, drinking his brother's blood. *Why was it drinking Josh's blood?* Sam thought to himself. The hooded figure looked up and said, "You're next!"

Oscar Edwardson (10)
Wheatlands Primary School, Redcar

The Haunted Forest

In the dead of night, Becca saw shooting stars soaring through the sky. She heard owls hooting which echoed through the woods. Running like she was on air, she came to a glittery lake flowing freely in the wind. Suddenly she heard a twig snap. Turning around she saw nothing, she continued walking, feeling wary about her surroundings. However, she didn't know what was awaiting her... Becca worried and she started running slowly. Glancing behind her she panicked. It wasn't a person chasing her, it was the forest trees. Running quickly she saw a haunted castle. She gasped, "Oh no!"

Lucie Scott (11)
Wheatlands Primary School, Redcar

Timmy And The Lost Forest

In a mysterious forest Timmy was lost. He found a cave. He heard a roar. The creature woke rapidly and said, "Who woke me?"

Timmy started to run and screamed, "You can talk." Timmy stopped and thought, *if the monster has been living here for many years and the town and people are nearby why hasn't it damaged the town?*

The monster shouted, "Stop! I won't hurt you. I just want a friend."

Timmy stopped, turned around and looked into the dragon's eyes. He saw that he had made a true friend. The dragon went to school with Timmy.

Louie Bowstead (10)
Wheatlands Primary School, Redcar

The Abandoned Woods

Jake needed to go through the sinister woods to get home. Entering the sinister woods, hairs stood up on his arms. Spooked, he suddenly thought someone or something was watching him. The trees stood like soldiers protecting the animals. The woods were silent. Well, that was until Jake heard a moan in the distance. Hesitantly, he slowly walked towards the noise. Behind some bushes, the ghost with fire for eyes was sat on a rock. Jake went over to help but the ghost attacked barbarically. He went missing that night. In fear, nobody went near those perplexing woods again.

Anya Wales (10)
Wheatlands Primary School, Redcar

The Mythical Forest

Inside the mythical forest there were rivers and lakes and mystical creatures were drinking all of the water. All of the water was gone so the trees couldn't get any. The forest was dying. The werewolf was hoping that he could get water back into the rivers. The werewolf was determined to get the water before they all died of thirst. Luckily, the werewolf could dig, so he started digging deeper in the dried-up river to find more water. Finally, water started pouring into the river so the griffins, frogs and owls could all drink again. They would survive.

Katie Middleton (10)
Wheatlands Primary School, Redcar

The Girl Who Could Howl

Annie was on a camping trip with her friends in the woods. Typically, all her friends left her to cook. She heard rustling from the bushes. She decided to ignore it. Then she heard it again and this time she didn't think it was her friends so she went to investigate. Initially, she couldn't see anything so she looked again and found something strange. When she came out her friends were there and they noticed that she was being chased by a pack of wolves. Looking closer, her friends realised she wasn't being chased by wolves, she was a wolf...

Jessica Buggey (10)
Wheatlands Primary School, Redcar

A Magical Walk

A girl went on a walk, but this one was bound to be different. She was alone you see. Just minding her own business and looking for leaves to use for her school project. Without knowing, she wandered off the muddy path. The girl stumbled through a bush and found herself in a clearing. In the clearing was a gleaming portal. The girl decided not to go through. All of a sudden, the portal started pulling her through. Magically, Hermione appeared. She started to battle the portal. Once winning, she disappeared and the girl ran home and never returned again.

Rosie Winspear (11)

Wheatlands Primary School, Redcar

Amy's Adventure

Amy was walking through the woods behind her house on the way to school. Her dad said, "Don't go in the woods!" but Amy couldn't resist. She had seen something and followed it but it had disappeared.

"I'm tired," she said to herself so she sat in an oak tree and something happened. She was transported into a magical land. She saw strange creatures. She told one she wanted to get home so he took her to a special pond. Amy made a wish; to go home. She was transported back to the same place her adventure had started.

Katie Walker (10)

Wheatlands Primary School, Redcar

The Secret Feast

At midnight, the woods become festive. Trees overlook a grand table, filled with jam tarts and warm tea. Fluffy, stuffed animals feast upon the foods and sing merrily in a joyful mood. Water rushes beside the trees and gently comes upon the riverbank as teddies cross with rucksacks upon their backs. Every teddy waffles about how they escaped their owner's grip and every teddy listens. Only we teddies know about this gathering. It can't be secret forever, so if you go down to the woods tonight you're sure to be in for a surprise.

Ethan Robinson (10)
Wheatlands Primary School, Redcar

The Way To Wonderland

Maddie was looking for conkers when she saw something shining from a pile of leaves. She sorted through them to find a little wooden door with a shiny brass handle. As she neared closer she began to shrink. She was so small she could easily fit through the little wooden door. As she creaked open the door to have a peek her jaw dropped in awe. The world was wonderfully weird, there was a talking cat exactly like Alice in Wonderland! She turned around to notice the door had vanished. She was stuck in Wonderland. Will poor Maddie ever escape?

Dolly Kirwan (10)
Wheatlands Primary School, Redcar

Maze Trap

There once was a forest which had magical powers and was filled with evil spirits inside it. They have the power to control the place... The place is the dreaded maze. One step off the path you seek a horrific sight you'll see. When you're in there's no escape for the maze's path will forever change. But there's one chance where you can seek your revenge. You must find out patterns to the maze you see, there will be a prize. Oh, it's a surprise, just you see. You'll reach out and find out it's all a dream...

Jonah Tennant (10)
Wheatlands Primary School, Redcar

Harry And The Mystical Forest

Surrounded by the dark oak trees, Harry looked around; the world seemed to darken. The gusting wind made Harry shiver. The water from the dark, dirty lake was flowing unusually. As Harry started to walk again, he saw his true love laying on the ground, matches. Harry ran and ran to find his way home but he was truly lost in this mysterious forest. *All alone*, he thought.

The next morning Harry woke up in a cave, there was tons of oil in it. All of a sudden Harry started to hear things. It was the Junkbots, they wanted oil...

Sam Drinkhall (10)

Wheatlands Primary School, Redcar

The Search For A Blizzard Crystal

A monster wizard and his apprentice were looking for a new spell in their spellbook and they needed a blizzard crystal for it. He sent his apprentice to the enchanted forest. When Tom, his apprentice, went to retrieve the crystal he saw glowing mushrooms, he was amazed. He also saw something glowing in the cut up ahead. He pushed the pine leaves out of the way, it was what he was looking for, the blizzard crystal. It was guarded by a dragon. He used his small knowledge of spells to vanquish it. He took the crystal back to his master.

Oliver Hamilton (11)

Wheatlands Primary School, Redcar

The Friendly Monster

Arriving at the forest Emily and Molly set up their tents and went to sleep. Early that morning they went adventuring through the woods. Suddenly they heard a noise, it was getting closer and closer. Emily and Molly started running and the thing chased them. It grabbed them and they realised it was helping them. He was telling them that they were being chased by a pack of wolves who were very hungry. He ran and climbed a tree to help them. All of a sudden a wolf grabbed the monster and he fell. They suddenly awoke in their bedrooms.

Jaycie-Kay Duncan (11)
Wheatlands Primary School, Redcar

Jemima's Lesson

After arguing with her parents Jemima ran away to the forest she has always been banned from, it had been a while and loud thuds got closer and closer. Jemima felt sick with worry and ran as fast as a cheetah, nobody could stop her! Feeling tired, Jemima tripped over a rock, she tumbled around absolutely horrified and guess who it was... her mum and dad. They crossly took her back to their house. Let's just say after the telling off her parents gave her Jemima will never step foot anywhere near the forest by herself ever again.

Gracie Mansfield (10)
Wheatlands Primary School, Redcar

Lost In The Woods

One bitter, cold day, the class went on a school trip to the woods. When they arrived, the teacher asked them to get into partners. Phoebe and Lainey decided to go together. They got a bit peckish, so they opened up a packet of crisps. As they were walking they found themselves lost! Luckily, they dropped a few crisps when they were walking so it left a trail. They had to be quick though as the squirrels started nibbling on them. Finally, they found the class but realised they had been so quick the teacher didn't even notice!

Phoebe Webster (10)
Wheatlands Primary School, Redcar

The World Is Changing

Lilia was walking in the woods with her family when she noticed that the air suddenly stood still and she saw a wisp of gold smoke. Her parents disappeared into thin air! Now her parents were gone she ventured to the other side of the woods to find herself surrounded by sweets. A river of melted marshmallows, chocolate trees and gummy leaves for her to eat until her heart's content. She ate the gummy leaves and felt fine and then she felt dizzy. When she woke up she found herself in a dark world, a world she did not like...

Sophie Marshall (10)
Wheatlands Primary School, Redcar

The End

As they ran from the end of the world, Bagel the cat and Karl, ran into the magical forest. They're safe but it's only them left in the world. They were wondering how they're going to live with no food, no drinks. They could not live in this state. They had no shelter. All of a sudden they heard a squawk-squawk in the trees above them. They saw a bird that was rainbow. They followed it and then saw a light. They saw lots of cats. All of a sudden Bagel said, "This is where we're going to live forever."

Louis Hartley (10)
Wheatlands Primary School, Redcar

Spooky Story

Jimmy and his family were going camping at the weekend. All around there were spirits and shadows in the woods around the eerie campsite. Jimmy went for a wander round the woods. Sounds were creeping from behind him. In the deep, dark woods trees were shaking, a light was in front, a campsite? Jimmy couldn't find his way back to the camp. Suddenly, around the corner a loud growl, monsters surrounded him. He knew he was being followed. There was a mountain behind him and then there was a loud roar from the mountain cave...

Theo Ward (10)

Wheatlands Primary School, Redcar

Mysterious Hidden World

Luna and her horse Moonlight were trotting in the woods. Luna knew there were a few branches in the forest but they jumped over them. On the way back she saw a hidden world in the bush so they went in. They loved it. Mysterious forest animals were running around. The sun was beginning to set so they were trying to find a way out.

Twenty minutes later she knew that they were lost. Luna shouted, "Let us out," and they were back in the woods again. When they were out they galloped home and told her mum about it.

Alexis Tate (10)
Wheatlands Primary School, Redcar

The Boy Who Flew

Max ran and ran through the trees without a care in the world. The trees started to thin as he neared the cliff edge; he kept on running and the trail became air. He neared the bottom but somehow he flapped his arms and started to fly over the trees and over the lakes. A hiker would've thought they were dreaming. The golden sun hung above the National Park. He ascended over the trail he first jumped off, he floated over until he was ready to land. Gently he touched down on the rough dirt. He would return tomorrow...

Callum Clegg (11)
Wheatlands Primary School, Redcar

An Enchanted Wood

Andy and his family are going through some woods camping and for a little bit of fun. They start walking and they realise they're starting to not know where they're going. As they think they see the campsite monsters surround them. They run away but they get lost. Soon after, the monsters find them and try to eat them but Andy and his family lead them into a trap. They run in a building and run back out and lock the monsters in. Next they find the campsite and all of them make a decision. Do they want to stay?

Ben Joseph Reed (10)
Wheatlands Primary School, Redcar

Monster Game

Alice was sat by the campfire one night, cold and alone, until she heard a deep, growling sound that sent a shiver down her spine. She stood up and ran as fast as she could into the forest, the monster still chasing her. It seemed big and definitely scary. After a long time of running she tripped over a large root as if the trees were against her. There it was, a big, blue, hairy monster running up to her. It tapped her and said, "Tig," in a girlish voice. She then realised she was just playing tig again...

Freya Putson (11)

Wheatlands Primary School, Redcar

The Rebirth Of Stickman

A lonely twig called Twig Man went for a stroll with his stick dog. His dog got lost in a bush so he followed but fell and found a note. 'To find your dog you're going to have to solve these clues... The first one is high or tall, you cannot find it low or small'. He went to the watchtower, it wasn't there so he went to the lighthouse. He found it in the clogs. It said, 'If you go back to your house you will be shocked beyond your eyes'. So he went... "Happy birthday," Grandad said.

Fabio Bernard (11)
Wheatlands Primary School, Redcar

The Heinous Unicorn

The campers arrived at the camp set up and then they found a bottle of water. One drinks the water and an evil unicorn appeared. The heinous unicorn tried to destroy the Earth with its horn. In only a few days it turned into winter. One day before the heinous unicorn finished destroyed the Earth, they found a book. It had a spell. It worked. The heinous unicorn had gone but not for long. The children grew up and told their children but they never believed it. They went camping and they found a bottle of water...

Annabelle Pearson (10)
Wheatlands Primary School, Redcar

Ghost Boy

As they sat around the campfire near the haunted wood a man started to tell the story of the wood. It was about a boy who got lost there and became a ghost who couldn't leave.

Later that night the eldest boy got some breadcrumbs and went into the wood and got lost. He found the ghost who explained that if accompanied by the boy when leaving he could turn to normal forever, but the breadcrumbs were gone. However, the boy remembered the way out so they got out and the ghost became a boy and was adopted.

Isaac Bilton (10)
Wheatlands Primary School, Redcar

Stickman

In a mysterious forest there lived a friendly stickman. One day, he decided to go out to fetch some sticks. Eventually, he found a huge pile, but as soon as he was about to pick them up a fox took them. He couldn't believe what had just happened, so decided to go back home. As soon as he was about to open the door, the fox came over with the sticks. The stickman was so pleased he decided to share the sticks with the fox. The fox explained that the only reason he took the sticks was to make friends...

Alfie McDonald (11)

Wheatlands Primary School, Redcar

The Two Lego Men

It all started when two Lego men went on a picnic. The sun went down very fast. The Lego men walked into a deep, dark wood. They kept walking for miles. That was when they found a tiny cottage full of little Lego people. They walked in the cottage and there was a Lego girl sat in the kitchen making lovely Lego pies. The two Lego men asked if they could have some. It turned out they had ten after that. After they set off the Lego girl shouted, "Do you want to stay? We are moving out soon."

Charlie Leach (10)

Wheatlands Primary School, Redcar

The Walk In The Forest

It's night-time and a group of friends are walking through the forest. Suddenly behind them a strange noise was heard and it came closer. The group then started to search the area but there was nothing there. The group heard it again but this time it was following them so they started dashing but it still followed them. Reaching for the end of the forest the strange noise turned into a shout. It turned out that the shout was one of the friend's mum who was trying to give her lunch to her.

Ruby Hodgson (11)
Wheatlands Primary School, Redcar

A Wander In The Woods

"At last we've arrived. This school bus is slower than I thought. It took over three hours to get to the forest." My classmates and I came off the bus and followed Mr Pendesen. We were walking along the path when I fell into a hole. I was confused... but once I realised what had happened, I had fallen into a cave, I looked up. There was no hole where I had fallen from. I put the light on my phone and found a ladder going to a trapdoor. Once out I regrouped with my classmates.

Reece Cummings (11)
Wheatlands Primary School, Redcar

The Dark Woods

Once there was a boy who set foot in an enchanted forest where none ever entered. As the boy walked further into the dark woods he saw talking trees and bushes, they turned around and said hello, then the boy fainted. When he woke up and the tree said do you want to have a party the boy said yes. So they went to an ancient house. They had a party. The boy heard a wolf stalking them so they ran. The wolf wanted the boy so the trees and bushes protected him but the wolf ate his head off!

Lloyd Johnson (10)
Wheatlands Primary School, Redcar

The Well

A lost little girl walks through the woods and comes upon a well, she cast a wish on the well and she gets transported to the Shadow Realm. She walks around but she gets captured by the shadow king. She breaks free and tries to escape but the shadow king finds her and turns her into a doll. So if you go down to the woods don't go at night because he will get you and you'll be in for a surprise. I suggest not going because you wouldn't want that to happen to you, would you?

Scarlett Scrafton (10)
Wheatlands Primary School, Redcar

The Forest

I woke up on a summer afternoon at summer camp with my friends. Just like any other morning it was my turn to get the water. I put on some clothes and ran out with the water bag. When I found a clear lake I knew something was off but I shook the feeling off and filled the bag. I then saw two monsters, one behind a tree. I felt my adrenaline race as I started to run. They chased me to camp. One stayed behind. I noticed it was my friend. I wondered who the other demonic monster was...

Luca Smith (11)
Wheatlands Primary School, Redcar

Aliens Invade

When I was wandering in the woods I saw a friendly, flying dragon and he took me through some black smoke. I then saw some yellow, green and red alien soldiers marching miles towards us. It turns out they were going to their boss/king. He likes to take over places. He has taken over all of the planets in the universe except Earth. I started to record it and everyone in the world saw it so everyone came and fought all of the aliens and we beat them. Their king went back to space.

Daniel Bryce (10)
Wheatlands Primary School, Redcar

Magical Frozen Puddle

One day in the frosty woods I saw a puddle of ice. I couldn't resist but to slide in it. I felt myself falling down and down. I stopped and saw a mystical place, a frosty world. I saw a village and heard a bark from behind me, it was a hungry wolf pack. I ran to the village as fast as I could. The wolves chased me. I couldn't see them anymore. I found a magic portal, it was glowing. I went through and the portal shut behind me. I was back in the woods, then I went home.

Cory Noble (10)

Wheatlands Primary School, Redcar

From Boy To Ghost

One day on a camping trip, my family and I went into a forest to get some firewood. After we found the firewood I went back to camp. When we got back we set up the tents, then I went to get stones for around the fire. When I returned I found the fire lit and a seat empty for me. As I sat we began telling ghost stories. When it came to my turn I wasn't human anymore, then I saw several other ghosts around me. I was told to find an elderly ghost, then I would be returned...

Bryn Boswell (10)
Wheatlands Primary School, Redcar

Ben And The Ghost

Entering the haunted forest, Ben, who went home through the forest, was walking quickly. As he glanced behind him he saw a psychopathic ghost on a horse with fire soaring from its eyes. Ben ran as fast as ever away from it but it kept chasing him home. He kept on running, he was coming to the edge of the forest. He could see the house from here so he kept running until he fell into a hole. There were lots of skeletons and gold but then his mum woke him up. It was a dream!

Archie Hodgson (10)

Wheatlands Primary School, Redcar

The Magical Forest

When Jack went into the woods he heard an owl hooting and there was a rapid river blocking his exit so he continued on. Suddenly he fell down a deep hole and he ended up breaking his leg and then he fell asleep. He was then helped out of the deep, long hole by goblins. The goblins set some more traps so other people could be trapped. The goblins started to eat Jack's blood and skin. The goblins then went to see if there were any more people trapped and there were...

Harvey Barton (11)
Wheatlands Primary School, Redcar

Lego Man

We were out having a great time in the woods. The girls were making daisy chains and the boys were playing hide-and-seek. We got tired so we decided to pack up in a rush. The boys and girls dropped me and didn't notice so they ran off in a hurry. Now I am stuck in a pile of leaves and mud. Will they find me, their little Lego Man? Have you ever been left in a dirty, old and gruesome forest all on your own with no way out? Would you find a way out if you were stuck?

Neve Pettite (10)

Wheatlands Primary School, Redcar

The Teddy Bears And The Ghost

It was midnight when we were finally able to slip away. We winked at the owl and saluted the old oak tree. With our picnic in our hands and a picnic table in our sight we came across a ghost! We managed to sneak past it but realised it was following us. We ran but it was too fast for us. Was it going to get us? No, instead all it wanted was to play, so we played till we couldn't anymore. We had our picnic and decided to go home. We all lived happily ever after.

Finley Mapplebeck (11)
Wheatlands Primary School, Redcar

The Haunted Woods

I can remember the day I became lost in the woods. I called my friends. As they showed up they found me but then they got lost too. An eerie sound echoed around them, as a ghostly shadow appeared to one of the group, we were all trembling with fear. A silvery outline glided in front of our terrified group. We built up the courage and went to have a look around. We took a torch and a ghost detector to see if there was a ghost but it was my dad to take me home.

Connor Sowerby (10)
Wheatlands Primary School, Redcar

The Never-Ending Dream

Suddenly everything stopped as I gazed at the stilled air. From the corner of my eye I saw a seven-legged creature with dreadful claws. Without a doubt, I ran. Breathing heavily I was still certain of survival but where to go? It was like I couldn't get away, every turn and every second he was still behind me. Eventually I lost him or so I thought but he had captured me and I had nowhere left to go and could do nothing but it had all just been a dream.

Lucas Richardson (10)

Wheatlands Primary School, Redcar

Stuck In A Fairy Tale

As I walked into the woods there was an arch tree guarding the woods. I went under and suddenly I fell into a fairy tale. When I woke up it still felt like a dream. In the distance, some crazy dwarves were staring at me and I was confused. I then realised that I was in Snow White but I needed to get home. I made my journey to the gingerbread man. Sadly everyone I asked said no and I have been here for I don't know how long. When will my story end...?

Darcie Cook (10)

Wheatlands Primary School, Redcar

Lost In The Woods

I can still remember the day that I became lost in the woods on a Year 6 trip. My friend and I wandered off into the gloomy trees... Time passed quickly as we played hide-and-seek. Suddenly, we were very scared. The woods are an unsuitable place for children after dark. We began sobbing when through the trees we heard a familiar voice calling our names, our teacher had found us! We all then realised how important it was not to wander off ever again.

Scarlett Willet

Wheatlands Primary School, Redcar

The Magical Forest

Once upon a time there was a sparkly, magical forest that was 50,000 years old! There was a special secret spirit that would amazingly protect the 50,000-year-old forest! The spirit protected the forest from the majestic wolves! The wolves would normally destroy the forest and kill the magical animals.

One incredibly shocking day the majestic wolves found a bright emerald stone that was glowing so bright it was brighter than the sun! Later the majestic wolves killed the spirit and the magical animals weren't magical now because the spirit had died. What will happen next...?

Maximus Roberts (9)

Ysgol Melyd, Prestatyn

Fairy Dust

Hello! My name is Annabelle! I've always dreamed of meeting a fairy. I even want to be one myself! I know my wish will not come true... but I still believe!
One day I went to a forest to collect some flowers. Suddenly I could hear sparkles and then wings flapping. As I was walking the forest became creepier and creepier... Suddenly the flowers started glowing, the birds started singing and bees started buzzing. I felt like I was in a story! As I walked back my mind thought, *could there be a fairy? If not, who is this person...?*

Maisie Vaughan (8)
Ysgol Melyd, Prestatyn

The Haunted Woods

It was a dark, stormy night when two kids went into the haunting, horrific woods so they could save their great-grandpa from thousands of ghosts! They arrived at their grandpa's. They opened the door and they saw their grandpa was tied up on the wall. They were scared and frightened. They untied him and he fell on the floor unconscious and bleeding! They screamed and called the police and an ambulance. The police came first and checked the house. The ambulance arrived and they brought out their grandpa but the kids were nowhere to be seen...

Noah Davies (9)

Ysgol Melyd, Prestatyn

The Magic Fairy

One day a fairy was in an enchanted forest. The fairy's name is Mill. She likes unicorns, I mean loves unicorns but one scary night when the fairy was sleeping an animal was shouting, "Let me in!" Mill went to the door to see who it was. In front of her was a magnificent unicorn staring right at her eyes! Mill said, "Hi, come in!"
The unicorn said, "Thank you!"
After that day they became best friends. They would go on walks, watch movies and other things that best friends do. Who is your best friend?

Sian Owen (8)

Ysgol Melyd, Prestatyn

Woods Killer Hunter

It was a spine-chilling morning when I took a step out my humongous house. I heard a loud scream, it sounded like it came from the creepy woods. I followed the noise, it was a girl screaming from the Woods Killer! We were absolutely terrified, we ran as fast as lightning! We found a big black cave, we stayed there for the night. We woke up and went for a walk, we found a mansion. All the doors were open, we went inside and nobody was there. We lived there forever because nobody came, so we lived happily ever after!

Will Lamb (8)

Ysgol Melyd, Prestatyn

The Worst Forest Ever

It was a horrible day in Speckletown and Susan was eating her breakfast. She escaped from her massive mansion. Susan went into the forest and saw a disguised robot from the future. She was paralysed with fear. The robot transformed into an evil vampire named Bob who was made by an evil spirit. Now she was shaking with fear. She just wanted to speed off like a cheetah. She tried to go the other way but couldn't pass the wall. She had to defeat Vampire Bob to pass the Wall of Doom. She tried a lot and passed...

Megan Duffy Hamill (9)
Ysgol Melyd, Prestatyn

The Mysterious Man And Creature

It was a glorious morning and I was told I had to go to the enchanted woods. I went to the woods like I was told. When I got there I stumbled upon a hideously, hairy creature. The creature stared for a moment then he chased me to a gigantic cage and locked me in. He smiled and laughed and walked away and never came back! I waited and waited but the creature was nowhere to be seen.

The next day the creature came back with a man, the man asked me, "What's your name?" I didn't answer...

Emily Hughes (8)
Ysgol Melyd, Prestatyn

The Scary Night

One day my friends and I went to the forest. Suddenly a black figure ran past. He was holding a dagger in his hand so my friends and I ran in fear. The next day I went back to the forest and there was nothing there except for a huge dragon so I ran to my friends' house and found them pale as a ghost. I told them about the fierce dragon and they told me that they didn't see it. Instead they had seen a black figure dragging a dripping bag. I shuddered in fear. What should I do?

Stanley Pope (8)
Ysgol Melyd, Prestatyn

The Mysterious Bear

Once upon a time a forbidden girl went into the dark and mysterious woods. In the distance she saw a gigantic house. It was called Spectacular Magnificent House, so she decided to go inside. She saw some porridge so she ate it. it was burning like a fire. She sat down on a tiny chair. Suddenly, she saw humongous footsteps, it was a huge bear. She sped out of the house like The Flash. She was home in a whiz. She went back to the woods, you won't believe what she saw...

Kian Semple (8)

Ysgol Melyd, Prestatyn

Wander In The Woods

They are in a humongous home! Their names are Jojo and James. They have powers. They go into the woods. Jojo goes left and James goes right. Jojo finds a magnificent fairy. She introduces herself. Her name is Summer.

Meanwhile, James finds a disgusting and grumpy ogre. He chases James. James bumps into Jojo. They use their powers but it seems impossible. Next they run home and hide in their beds but the ogre finds them...

Elijah Jones (9)

Ysgol Melyd, Prestatyn

YOUNG WRITERS INFORMATION

We hope you have enjoyed reading this book – and that you will continue to in the coming years.

If you're a young writer who enjoys reading and creative writing, or the parent of an enthusiastic poet or story writer, do visit our website **www.youngwriters.co.uk**. Here you will find free competitions, workshops and games, as well as recommended reads, a poetry glossary and our blog. There's lots to keep budding writers motivated to write!

If you would like to order further copies of this book, or any of our other titles, then please give us a call or order via your online account.

Young Writers
Remus House
Coltsfoot Drive
Peterborough
PE2 9BF
(01733) 890066
info@youngwriters.co.uk

Join in the conversation!
Tips, news, giveaways and much more!

 YoungWritersUK    @YoungWritersCW    @YoungWritersCW